Nature Did It First!

SUSAN E. GOODMAN

PHOTOGRAPHS BY
DOROTHY HANDELMAN

THE MILLBROOK PRESS
BROOKFIELD, CONNECTICUT

To Nature's Best—Ron, Diane, Jesse, Raffi, and Mrs. Diaz   SG
To Nora, Sarah, and Jacob   DH

Library of Congress Cataloging-in-Publication Data
Goodman, Susan E., 1952-
Nature did it first! / by Susan E. Goodman ; photographs by Dorothy Handelman.
p. cm.
Summary: Photographs provide examples of human inventions that have been borrowed from nature.
ISBN 0-7613-2413-5 (lib. bdg.)
1. Nature—Miscellanea—Juvenile literature. [1. Nature—Miscellanea.] I. Handelman, Dorothy, ill. II. Title.
QH48 .G65 2003   508—dc21   2002014111

Photos on cover (top left, bottom right) and pages 3, 5, 7, 9, 11, 13, 15, 17, 19, 21 copyright © 2003 by Dorothy Handelman.
With special thanks to the Hargitai family, Khalil Jarane, Susan and Matthew Marshall, Neil Metcalf, Landon Parton,
Jennifer and Avery Schumacher, Juliet Semel, Katie Smercak, and the Handelman-West family.

Other photographs courtesy of Photo Researchers, Inc.: cover (bottom left) and p.10 © Patti Murray, pp. 4 (© Gregory
G. Dimijian), 6 (© Tom McHugh), 14 (© Gary Retherford), 18 (© Anthony Mercieca), 20 (© Alan D. Carey), 22 (© Scott
Camazine); Animals Animals: pp.1 (© Ken Cole), 2 (© Johnny Johnson), 8 (© Ana Laura Gonzalez), 16 (© Ken Cole), 24
(© Johnny Johnson); Visuals Unlimited, Inc.: cover (top right) and p. 12 © Jane Thomas.

Published by The Millbrook Press, Inc.
2 Old New Milford Road
Brookfield, Connecticut 06804
www.millbrookpress.com

Printed in the United States of America
1 3 5 4 2

Camouflage

$\mathcal{N}$ature did it first!

Spots and the color of its fur help the leopard hide while hunting.

Baby carrier

*N*ature did it first!

Joeys, baby kangaroos, live in their mothers' pouches for ten months after birth.

Shower

*N*ature did it first!

Elephants use their trunks to wash—also to eat, drink, smell, breathe, touch, and fight. Made up of 100,000 muscles, trunks can be strong enough to lift heavy logs and flexible enough to pick up a peanut.

Straw

*N*ature did it first!

Some moths and butterflies suck nectar through a long hollow tube called a proboscis. The drinking-straw tongue of this dotted skipper butterfly coils up when it is not being used.

Umbrella

Nature did it first!

In wet climates, some termite nests are protected by umbrella-shaped roofs, which make the rain spill off to the side.

Scissors

Nature did it first!

Leaf cutter ants use the leaves they cut up as soil to grow the fungus that they like to eat. Like all ants, their mandibles are a set of jaws that move sideways, not up and down like ours.

Spill-proof container

Nature did it first!

Eggshells protect what's inside, but they aren't solid.
Tiny holes called pores let air in so the developing chicks can grow.
These eggs will hatch into a family of scrub-jays.

Armor

Nature did it first!

The armadillo is the only mammal that has bones in its skin. Though some armadillos roll into a ball to protect themselves, most of them try to run or dig their way to safety.

Sleeping bag

*N*ature did it first!

A monarch caterpillar goes into its "sleeping bag" for much longer than one night. Its chrysalis keeps it warm and safe while it changes into a butterfly.

Family

Taking care of children is a part of nature . . .

. . . for penguins AND people.
People may take ideas from nature
to make helmets and juice boxes,
but we are a part of nature too.